MW01532748

A Word

to the

Wise

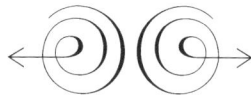

little bites of wisdom

from

Jason Perry

OAK TREE
LEADERSHIP

A Word to the Wise
little bites of wisdom from Jason Perry

Copyright © 2023 by Jason Perry

ISBN 979-8-3959-3206-8

For additional information, write
Oak Tree Leadership:
16000 Van Drunen Rd, South Holland, IL 60473
jperry12871@gmail.com
www.oaktree-leadership.com
Printed in the United States of America.

A Word from the Author

A movie trailer does not tell you the whole story, but just enough to get you interested to want to watch the movie. I want you to think of *A Word to the Wise* as a trailer for your own walk with the Lord. The thoughts contained here should elicit at least one of three responses:

- *Aha* - A new perspective on a familiar thought.
- *Uh-Oh* - A challenge to change behavior or mindset.
- *Hmm* - A catalyst for deeper reflection.

It is my prayer that you will be inspired to take your own relationship with God to higher levels as you seek to be known by Him, to know Him better, and to make Him known to others.

Jason Perry

What is the price of five sparrows—

two copper coins?

Yet God does not forget a single one of them.

And the very hairs on your head are all

numbered.

So don't be afraid; you are more valuable to God

than a whole flock of sparrows.

Luke 12:6

The value of a diamond

buried in the house of a hoarder

is not diminished by the mounds of clutter.

Regardless of the circumstances of your present

or the mistakes of your past,

you are still a person of infinite worth.

You are worth fighting for!

A third time He asked him,

Simon son of John,

do you love Me?

John 21:17

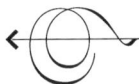

The Lord does not ask questions

in order to

gather information

for Himself,

but to reveal to us

our true selves.

The Lord is my strength and shield.

I trust Him with all my heart.

He helps me, and my heart is filled with joy.

I burst out in songs of thanksgiving.

Psalms 28:7

Don't let the negative

become your narrative.

Seed your life with gratitude

so that it does not become

overgrown with sadness.

"O Sovereign Lord," I said, "I can't speak for you! I'm too young!" The Lord replied, "Don't say, 'I'm too young,' for you must go wherever I send you

and say whatever I tell you."

Jeremiah 1:6

God does not speak

merely to inform,

but to transform

the one

to whom He is speaking.

He went on a little farther

and bowed with His face to the ground,

praying, "My Father! If it is possible,

let this cup of suffering be taken away from Me.

Yet I want your will to be done, not Mine."

Matthew 26:39

What grows in your garden?

In the garden of Eden,

man experienced his greatest failure—

the exaltation of his will above God's.

In the garden of Gethsemane,

the Son of Man experienced His greatest

triumph—

the submission of His will to God.

"For we must all stand

before Christ to be judged.

We will each receive

whatever we deserve for the good or evil

we have done in this earthly body."

2 Corinthians 5:10

Don't assume that the presence

of God's love and grace means

the absence of His holiness

and accountability.

Give all your worries and cares to God,

for He cares about you.

1 Peter 5:7

Share each other's burdens,

and in this way obey the law of Christ.

Galatians 6:2

∞

God carries our burdens

so our hands and hearts

are free to help

someone else

with theirs.

Three different times I begged the Lord to take it away. Each time he said, "My grace is all you need. My power works best in weakness." So now I am glad to boast about my weaknesses, so that the power of Christ can work through me.

2 Corinthians 12:8

Miracles.

Jesus turned water into wine.

God's grace turns

whine into power.

But I have pleaded in prayer

for you...

Luke 22:32

The best thing you can do

for a person

who is hurting

is to hold them up in prayer

so that God

can pour into them.

Jesus told him, "I am the way, the truth, and the life. No one can come to the Father except through Me."

John 14:6

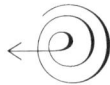

There are many paths

that lead to truths,

but there is only one person

*that is **The Truth**.*

We all fell down,

and I heard a voice saying to me in Aramaic,

'Saul, Saul, why are you persecuting Me?

It is useless for you to fight against my will.'

"'Who are you, lord?' I asked.

"And the Lord replied,

'I am Jesus, the One you are persecuting.

Acts 26:14

Ultimately, your fight is not

against other people or systems,

but against your own unwillingness

to admit that Jesus, not you,

is the Lord.

Search me, O God,

and know my heart;

test me

and know my anxious thoughts.

Point out anything in me that offends You,

and lead me along the path of everlasting life.

Psalm 139:23-24

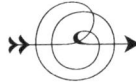

You not knowing

what will kill you

will kill you

before

you even know it.

But the jar he was making

did not turn out as he had hoped,

so he crushed it

into a lump of clay again

and started over.

Jeremiah 18:4

God sets us apart

in our impotence and inability

and then begins the arduous process

of reshaping our character so that we may

be used for His purpose and glory.

Jesus knew that the Father had given him

authority over everything and

that he had come from God

and would return to God.

So he got up from the table, took off his robe,

wrapped a towel around his waist,

and poured water into a basin.

Then he began to wash the disciples' feet,

drying them with the towel he had around him.

John 13:3-5

Are you secure enough

in your identity in Christ

to be able

to help someone else find theirs?

So to keep me from becoming proud,

I was given a thorn in my flesh,

a messenger from Satan

to torment me

and keep me from becoming proud.

2 Cor. 12:7

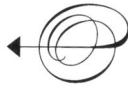

There is no sharpening without friction,

and there is no strengthening

without resistance.

Embrace both because

God is using them to make you better.

But Samuel replied,

"What is more pleasing to the Lord:

your burnt offerings and sacrifices

or your obedience to His voice?

Listen!

Obedience is better than sacrifice,

and submission is better

than offering the fat of rams.

1 Samuel 15:22

Simple acts of humble obedience

are better

than grand displays

of insincere sacrifice.

What can we bring to the Lord?

Should we bring Him burnt offerings?

Should we bow before God Most High

with offerings of yearling calves?

No, O people,

the Lord has told you what is good,

and this is what He requires of you:

to do what is right, to love mercy,

and to walk humbly with your God.

Micah 6:6,8

Insincere sacrifices

are outward religious activities

that do not reflect

your true inner spiritual reality.

Remain in me, and I will remain in you.

For a branch cannot produce fruit

if it is severed from the vine,

and you cannot be fruitful

unless you remain in me.

John 15:4

Learn to walk

in such intimacy with God

that He doesn't have to

make an appointment

to reach you.

And now, dear brothers and sisters,

we want you to know what will happen

to the believers who have died

so you will not grieve

like people who have no hope.

I Thessalonians 4:13

Loss leaves a hole in your life.

Good grieving is learning

how to put up guardrails

that allow you to approach the hole

without falling into it.

This is My command—

be strong and courageous!

Do not be afraid or discouraged.

For the Lord your God is with you

wherever you go.

Joshua 1:9

Courage is not the absence of fear.

Courage is the absolute confidence

in the power, presence,

provision, purpose

and protection of God.

Share each other's burdens,

and in this way

obey the law of Christ.

Galatians 6:2

It's okay

to ask for help.

When you're stuck,

it's hard

to push and drive

at the same time.

For just as the heavens

are higher than the earth,

so My ways are higher than your ways

and My thoughts higher than your thoughts.

Isaiah 55:9

Your inability

to understand or to explain

does not invalidate

what God says,

who He is

or what He does.

You have been believers so long now

that you ought to be teaching others.

Instead, you need someone to teach you again

the basic things about God's word.

You are like babies who need milk

and cannot eat solid food.

Hebrews 5:12

⌘

Our experiences are mistakes

only when we fail to learn from them

or help somebody else

because of them.

"You won't die!"

the serpent replied to the woman.

"God knows

that your eyes will be opened

as soon as you eat it,

and you will be like God,

knowing both good and evil."

Genesis 3:4-5

Beware the enemy's power

to deceive and destroy.

He convinced Adam and Eve

to trade their souls

to gain something they already possessed—

being like God.

Seek the Kingdom of God above all else,

and live righteously,

and He will give you

everything you need.

Matthew 6:33

You give highest priority

to that failure

which has

the greatest consequence.

Before daybreak the next morning,

Jesus got up

and went out to an isolated place to pray.

When they found Him, they said,

"Everyone is looking for You."

But Jesus replied,

"We must go on to other towns as well, and I

will preach to them, too. That is why I came."

Mark 1:35

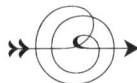

Prayerfully discerned purpose

prevents pressure

from problems, peers

and personal ego.

Zacchaeus quickly climbed down

and took Jesus to his house

in great excitement and joy.

But the people were displeased.

"He has gone to be the guest

of a notorious sinner," they grumbled.

Luke 19:6

Jesus was willing to risk

the wrath of the righteous

in order to win

the souls of sinners.

So the next generation might know them—

even the children not yet born—

and they in turn

will teach their own children.

Psalms 78:6

An impactful life

is more like a relay race

than a sprint.

You only win

when your efforts

help others win.

Why am I discouraged?

Why is my heart so sad?

I will put my hope in God!

I will praise Him again—

my Savior and my God...

Psalms 42:5-6

Feelings are the caboose of the train.

If your life is being led by the caboose

and not the engine of faith in the truth,

you are probably out of control.

"Simon, Simon,

Satan has asked to sift each of you like wheat.

But I have pleaded in prayer for you, Simon,

that your faith should not fail.

So when you have repented and turned to Me

again, strengthen your brothers." Luke 22:31

∿

Your failures don't have to be fatal.

What describes you

does not have to define you.

Your detours

don't have to be your final destination.

After they had been severely flogged,

they were thrown into prison,

and the jailer was commanded

to guard them carefully.

When he received these orders,

he put them in the inner cell

and fastened their feet in the stocks.

About midnight Paul and Silas were praying

and singing hymns to God,

and the other prisoners were listening to them.

Acts 16:23-25 (NIV)

One measure of spiritual maturity

is the distance between the onset of problems

and the onset of peace.

To the weak I became weak, to win the weak. I

have become all things to all people so that by

all possible means I might save some.

I do all this for the sake of the gospel,

that I may share in its blessings.

I Corinthians 9:22-23 (NIV)

We must use

ever-changing methodologies

to reach

an ever-changing culture

with the

never-changing Gospel of Jesus Christ.

Trust in the Lord with all your heart;

do not depend on your own understanding.

Seek His will in all you do,

and He will show you which path to take.

Proverbs 3:5

Instead of asking God

to bless your plans,

ask Him

to give you the plans

that He will bless.

You are the light of the world—

like a city on a hilltop

that cannot be hidden.

Matthew 5:14

Light is more powerful than darkness.

If the darkness

is overshadowing your light,

either you are absent

from the darkness

or the light is absent from you.

"...Father, forgive them,

for they don't know what they are doing...

...I assure you,

today you will be with Me in paradise..."

When Jesus saw His mother standing there

beside the disciple He loved, He said to her,

"Dear woman, here is your son."

Luke 23:34,43; John 19:26

Jesus loved FROM the cross.

He did not wait to feel better to do better.

He prayed, cared, and served others

in the midst

of His pain, suffering, and loss.

Can anything ever

separate us from Christ's love?

Does it mean He no longer loves us

if we have trouble or calamity,

or are persecuted, or hungry, or destitute,

or in danger, or threatened with death?

Romans 8:35

The presence of problems

does not necessarily

indicate

the absence of God.

"I am the true grapevine,

and My Father is the gardener.

He cuts off every branch of Mine

that doesn't produce fruit,

and He prunes the branches that do bear fruit

so they will produce even more.

John 15:1

The enemy of the best

is not the bad, but the good.

Don't spend your life doing good.

Invest your life doing what is best.

Let the wise listen to these proverbs
and become even wiser.

Let those with understanding receive
guidance...

Proverbs 1:5

Anything worth doing

is worth doing poorly.

It is better to attempt

and then improve by learning from your

mistakes than to be perfectly inactive

and remain the same.

Work willingly at whatever you do,

as though you were working

for the Lord rather than for people.

Colossians 3:23

The quality, faithfulness and duration

of your service

should not be determined

by your commitment to a leader or a

cause, but by your passion for

and submission to the Lord.

But the Holy Spirit produces

this kind of fruit in our lives:

love, joy, peace, patience,

kindness, goodness, faithfulness...

Galatians 5:22

❦

Faithfulness flows

from a person's character.

Therefore, it can be modeled, mimicked,

manifested and mentored, but it cannot

be mandated.

Put on your new nature,

and be renewed

as you learn to know your Creator

and become like Him.

Colossians 3:10

Is your faith

more like the clothes

you wear

or the skin

in which you live?

And God will generously provide

all you need.

Then you will always have

everything you need

and plenty left over

to share with others.

2 Corinthians 9:8

What gifts

has God given you

to change the world?

Then as I looked over the situation,

I called together the nobles and the rest of the

people and said to them, "Don't be afraid of the

enemy! Remember the Lord, Who is great and

glorious,

and fight for your brothers, your sons,

your daughters, your wives, and your homes!"

Nehemiah 4:14

When facing discouragement,

remember...

...who you are fighting against.

...Who is fighting for you.

...who you are fighting for.

...Miriam died and was buried...

...they rebelled against Moses and Aaron...

Then Moses raised his hand

and struck the rock twice with the staff...

But the Lord said to Moses and Aaron,

"Because you did not trust Me

enough to demonstrate my holiness

to the people of Israel, you will not lead them

into the land I am giving them!"

Numbers 20:1

*Never make significant decisions
when you are
sad, tired, and/or angry.*

Take My yoke upon you. Let Me teach you,

because I am humble and gentle at heart,

and you will find rest for your souls.

Matthew 11:29

God, help me to not run ahead of You

in creative impetuousness

or to lag behind You in emotional fear.

But let my soul be yoked up with You

so that I may walk with You

at Your pace

in the unforced rhythms of grace.

And now, dear brothers and sisters,

we want you to know what will happen

to the believers who have died

so you will not grieve

like people who have no hope.

1 Thessalonians 4:13

⚜

Having a proper theology

about what happens after we die

is a key factor

in having peace

while we are living.

This is My command—

be strong...Joshua 1:9

I do not ask God to **USE** my strength

because I have none.

I don't ask Him to **GIVE** me strength

because I would misuse or misplace it.

I ask him to **BE** my strength

because then I will have

whatever I need,

for whenever I need it,

for however long I need it.

And you should imitate me,

just as I imitate Christ.

1 Corinthians 11:1

Car-i-ca-ture

"a picture, description, or imitation

of a person in which certain striking

characteristics are exaggerated in order to

create a comic or grotesque effect."

I wonder how often people are rejecting

our **caricature** *of Christ as opposed*

to the **character** *of Christ?*

The faithful love of the Lord never ends!

His mercies never cease.

Great is His faithfulness;

His mercies begin afresh each morning.

Lamentations 3:22-23

God's grace is displayed in God's...

...Unchanging positive attitude

towards us.

...Unconditional love

for us.

...Unparalleled power

to accomplish what He desires for us.

He forgives all my sins

and heals all my diseases.

He redeems me from death

and crowns me with love and tender mercies.

He fills my life with good things.

My youth is renewed like the eagle's!

Psalm 103:3-5

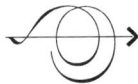

Abiding in God's grace

gives us the capacity

to mess up, fess up,

and move on.

We now have this light shining in our hearts,

but we ourselves

are like fragile clay jars

containing this great treasure.

This makes it clear

that our great power is from God,

not from ourselves.

2 Corinthians 4:7

❁

Allow your brokenness

to keep you humble,

but do not let it make you mute.

Remember that a cracked mirror

can still reflect light.

The Lord said to Gideon,

"You have too many warriors with you.

If I let all of you fight the Midianites,

the Israelites will boast to Me

that they saved themselves

by their own strength." Judges 7:2

Sometimes God adds to us

by subtracting something from us.

I've learned to trust

that His math is better than mine.

Yes, everything else is worthless

when compared with the infinite value

of knowing Christ Jesus my Lord.

For His sake I have discarded everything else,

counting it all as garbage,

so that I could gain Christ. Philippians 3:7-9

What is our purpose?

- *To be known by God.*

- *To know God.*

- *To make God known.*

If you keep yourself pure,

you will be a special utensil for honorable use.

Your life will be clean,

and you will be ready

for the Master to use you for every good work.

2 Timothy 2:21

Calling is to purpose

what a flashlight is to a battery:

It is the means, setting, or activity

that releases the potential

already stored within you.

Don't you realize

that in a race everyone runs,

but only one person gets the prize?

So run to win!

1 Corinthians 9:24

Success is

identifying the unique purpose

for which you have been created

and then giving your life

to turning that potential

into reality.

All athletes are disciplined in their training.

They do it to win a prize that will fade away,

but we do it for an eternal prize.

So I run with purpose in every step.

I am not just shadowboxing.

1 Corinthians 9:25

❧

Without purpose,

routines can become ruts

instead of roads.

Not that I was ever in need,

for I have learned how to be content

with whatever I have.

I know how to live on almost nothing

or with everything.

I have learned the secret of living in every

situation, whether it is

with a full stomach or empty,

with plenty or little.

For I can do everything through Christ,

Who gives me strength.   Philippians 4:11-13

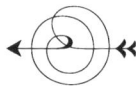

Contentment is not the absence of ambition,

but the deep sense of gratitude

for the present provision of my God

Who loves me and knows what I need.

For a child is born to us,

a son is given to us.

The government will rest

on His shoulders... Isaiah 9:6

Jesus is more than a baby in a manger,

a good teacher, or a cultural icon.

He is a revolutionary who has come

to turn the world right side up

after the enemy has turned it

upside down.

Get wisdom, get understanding;

do not forget my words

or turn away from them.

Proverbs 4:5 (NIV)

The only chance you have

of not carrying your negative past

into your tomorrow

is to not pack it

in the luggage of the decisions

that you make today.

...Let us strip off every weight

that slows us down,

especially the sin that so easily trips us up.

And let us run with endurance

the race God has set before us.

Hebrews 12:1

Having a goal

without having a plan to achieve it

and the perseverance to pursue it

is like seeing the mountain's peak,

but failing to see the mountain.

Trust in the Lord with all your heart;

do not depend on your own understanding.

Seek His will in all you do,

and He will show you which path to take.

Proverbs 3:5-6

Living your life

on the basis of emotions

is like building your house

on the surface of the ocean.

From the tribe of Issachar, there were

200 leaders of the tribe with their relatives.

All these men understood

the signs of the times

and knew the best course for Israel to take.

I Chronicles 12:32

We are living in complex times

with complex problems

that require complex solutions.

Are you engaging in critical thinking,

or are you just critical in your thinking?

But Samuel said, "What is this you have done?"

Saul replied,

"I saw my men scattering from me,

and you didn't arrive when you said you would,

and the Philistines are at Micmash ready for

battle..." "How foolish!" Samuel exclaimed.

"You have not kept the command

the Lord your God gave you..."

1 Samuel 13:11, 13

❧

Faithless peers,

personal fears and powerful foes

are never adequate justifications

for disobedience to God.

For you are all children of the light

and of the day;

we don't belong to darkness and night.

So be on your guard,

not asleep like the others.

Stay alert and be clearheaded.

I Thessalonians 5:5-6

*What troubles me more
than the world being dark
is the church not being light.*

...I am Joseph, your brother,

whom you sold into slavery in Egypt.

But don't be upset,

and don't be angry with yourselves

for selling me to this place.

It was God who sent me here ahead of you

to preserve your lives.   Genesis 45:4-5

Reorienting our vision

to see our lives through the lens

of God's grace and sovereignty

creates a pathway of healing

that changes

how we view God,

our experiences, ourselves, and others.

Dear friends, never take revenge.

Leave that to the righteous anger of God.

For the Scriptures say, "I will take revenge;

I will pay them back," says the Lord.

Instead, "If your enemies are hungry, feed them.

If they are thirsty,

give them something to drink.

In doing this, you will heap

burning coals of shame on their heads."

Don't let evil conquer you, but conquer evil

by doing good.   Romans 12:19-21

*Grudges **ENSLAVE***

*Revenge **KILLS***

*Kindness **HEALS***

"No, don't be afraid.

I will continue to take care

of you and your children."

So, he reassured them

by speaking kindly to them.

Genesis 50:21

Kindness is the practice

of speaking

to a person's heart

regardless of the behavior

of their hands.

GRAyCE SPACE

Recognize the value of every person

and continually show love to every believer.

Live your lives with great reverence

and in holy awe of God.

Honor your rulers.   1 Peter 2:17 (TPT)

Very often, our relationships and interactions

don't fall into neat extremes

of BLACK or WHITE, YES or NO,

but in the challenging ground

somewhere in-between.

It is in this **GRAyCE SPACE**

where we need to operate

in the greatest measures

of love, wisdom, humility and Godliness.

Let your conversation

be always full of grace,

seasoned with salt,

so that you may know

how to answer everyone.

Colossians 4:6 (NIV)

The **GRAyCE SPACE** is that space between

unbending positions where...

...we can disagree

without being disagreeable.

...arguments don't end relationships.

The godly may trip seven times,

but they will get up again...

Proverbs 24:16

*The **GRAyCE SPACE** is that space*

between unbending positions where...

...you have the permission to try and fail

...multiple times.

...you can fail or lose

without being labeled

or labeling yourself as a failure or loser.

And you will know the truth,

and the truth will set you free.

John 8:32

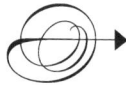

The **GRAyCE SPACE** *is that space between*

unbending positions where...

...holding convictions

does not mean you are intolerant.

...expressing truth

does not equal hate speech.

Then Peter came to Jesus and asked,

"Lord, how many times shall I forgive

my brother or sister who sins against me?

Up to seven times?"

Jesus answered, "I tell you, not seven times,

but seventy-seven times."

Matthew 18:21-22 (NIV)

The GRAyCE SPACE is that space

between unbending positions where...

...the benefit of the doubt is given.

...forgiveness is extended freely.

Never pay back evil with more evil.

Do things in such a way

that everyone can see you are honorable.

Do all that you can

to live in peace with everyone.

Romans 12:17-18

The GRAyCE SPACE is that space

between unbending positions where...

...vulnerability, opinion, and truth

are not weaponized.

Give, and it will be given to you.

A good measure, pressed down,

shaken together and running over,

will be poured into your lap.

For with the measure you use,

it will be measured to you.   Luke 6:38 (NIV)

The GRAyCE SPACE is that space

between unbending positions where...

...the amount of rope we give to others

reflects the amount of rope

we have been given ourselves.

I tell you, this sinner, not the Pharisee,

returned home justified before God.

For those who exalt themselves

will be humbled,

and those who humble themselves

will be exalted.

Luke 18:14

The **GRAyCE SPACE** is that space between

unbending positions where...

...being righteous

is more important than being right.

Dear brothers and sisters,

if another believer is overcome by some sin,

you who are godly should gently and humbly

help that person back onto the right path. And

be careful not to fall

into the same temptation yourself.

Galatians 6:1

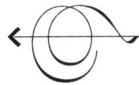

The GRAyCE SPACE is that space

between unbending positions where...

...accountability

is not considered judgment.

Confess your sins to each other

and pray for each other

so that you may be healed.

The earnest prayer of a righteous person

has great power

and produces wonderful results.   James 5:16

*The **GRAyCE SPACE** is that space*

between unbending positions where...

...the confession of sin produces prayer,

not shade or shame.

Let all who are spiritually mature

agree on these things.

If you disagree on some point,

I believe God will make it plain to you.

But we must hold on to the progress

we have already made.   Philippians 3:15-16

The GRAyCE SPACE is that space

between unbending positions where...

...we praise the presence of progress,

rather than

condemn the absence of perfection.

Then Jesus stood up again

and said to the woman,

"Where are your accusers?

Didn't even one of them condemn you?"

"No, Lord," she said.

And Jesus said,

"Neither do I. Go and sin no more."

John 8:10

The **GRAyCE SPACE** is that space

between unbending positions where...

...love covers a multitude of sin,

but sin is not ignored

in the name of love.

Looking at the man, Jesus felt genuine love for him. "There is still one thing you haven't done," He told him.

"Go and sell all your possessions

and give the money to the poor,

and you will have treasure in heaven.

Then come, follow Me."

Mark 10:21

*The **GRAyCE SPACE** is that space between*

unbending positions where...

...uncompromised convictions

and unconditional love

are not mutually exclusive.

The woman was surprised, for Jews refuse

to have anything to do with Samaritans.

She said to Jesus, "You are a Jew,

and I am a Samaritan woman.

Why are you asking me for a drink?"

John 4:9

The GRAyCE SPACE is that space

between unbending positions where...

...in the times of dispute,

we chose conversation over

cancellation.

Moses'
Masterclass

At that time Moses was born—

a beautiful child in God's eyes.

His parents cared for him at home

for three months.

Acts of the Apostles 7:20

❦

In his life, Moses was ...born during a genocide

...abandoned by his parents

...adopted into and raised in a hostile environment

...rejected as a leader...homeless.

He had identity issues and committed a felony.

God, not your circumstances or

environment, establishes your value.

Moses was taught

all the wisdom of the Egyptians,

and he was powerful in both speech

and action.   Acts of the Apostles 7:22

Bloom where you are planted.

Instead of lamenting

about where you are not,

decide to use the time and resources

available to you where you are

to help you become

who God created you to be.

91

He saw an Egyptian mistreating an Israelite.

So Moses came to the man's defense

and avenged him, killing the Egyptian.

Moses assumed his fellow Israelites

would realize that God had sent him

to rescue them, but they didn't.

Acts of the Apostles 7:24

Always seek alignment with God.
What appears to make sense to us
does not always make sense to God.
Prayerfully choose your course of action
so that it aligns with the heart of God.

When Moses heard that, he fled the country

and lived as a foreigner in the land of Midian.

There his two sons were born.

Acts of the Apostles 7:29

Don't settle for Midian.

Midian represents being satisfied

with what is within our reach,

rather than yielding to God

so that He can make us

who He wants us to become.

"I am the God of your fathers,

the God of Abraham, Isaac and Jacob."

Moses trembled with fear

and did not dare to look.

Acts of the Apostles 7:32 NIV

Ask God the right questions.

In challenging times,

instead of asking God,

"Where are you?" or "Why me?",

ask Him, "What are You teaching me?"

"What do You want me to teach others?"

Forty years later,

in the desert near Mount Sinai,

an angel appeared to Moses

in the flame of a burning bush.

Acts of the Apostles 7:30

Don't despise the desert.

There is always a desert season of

PREPARATION

between the ANOINTING

—when God calls you—

and the APPOINTING—

when God uses you.

...An angel appeared to Moses

in the flame of a burning bush.

When Moses saw it,

he was amazed at the sight.

As he went to take a closer look,

the voice of the Lord called out to him...

Acts of the Apostles 7:30

Pay attention to God in the desert.

It is not until we turn aside

from our own agendas

that our ears and hearts can be available

to hear the voice of God.

I have indeed seen

the oppression of my people in Egypt.

I have heard their groaning

and have come down to set them free.

Now come, I will send you back to Egypt.

Acts of the Apostles 7:34, NIV

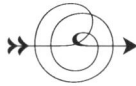

Walk in your anointing.

God's favor is upon you

to achieve something

of great significance for His Kingdom.

Don't be afraid of its bigness.

Embrace His grace on your life.

AUTHENTIC
WORSHIP

Then I said,

"It's all over! I am doomed,

for I am a sinful man.

I have filthy lips,

and I live among a people with filthy lips.

Yet I have seen the King,

the Lord of Heaven's Armies."   Isaiah 6:5

Authentic worship allows us to see

that God is not a part of our life,

*but God **IS** our life.*

We see our life in the context of God

Who does not need to prove His existence,

justify his presence,

or earn a place in our lives.

*God is not an add-on; **He is all!***

Then one of the seraphim flew to me

with a burning coal he had taken from the altar

with a pair of tongs.

He touched my lips with it and said,

"See, this coal has touched your lips.

Now your guilt is removed,

and your sins are forgiven."

Isaiah 6:6-7

Authentic worship opens the door

for Christ to be formed in us

by giving us a clear view

of the lengths to which

God went to recover, redeem and restore

His lost children.

Then I heard the Lord asking,

"Whom should I send

as a messenger to this people?

Who will go for us?"

I said, "Here I am. Send me."

Isaiah 6:8

Our response

to God's gracious redemptive, renewal

and renovative work in our lives

should be to submit to His leadership

and make ourselves available

to do His work.

One of them, when he saw that he was healed,

came back to Jesus, shouting, “Praise God!”

He fell to the ground at Jesus’ feet,

thanking Him for what He had done.

This man was a Samaritan.

Luke 17:15

A truly thankful heart

will propel us

beyond an arrogant and ignorant

sense of entitlement

to a posture

of humble acknowledgment.

Jesus asked, "Were not all ten cleansed?

Where are the other nine?

Has no one returned to give praise to God

except this foreigner?"

Then He said to him,

"Rise and go; your faith has made you well."

Luke 17:17-19 (NIV)

Receiving a gift can produce in us

a sense of happiness.

But a genuine attitude of gratitude

ignites in us healing

and a restoration of wholeness.

How do you wait on God?

Let all that I am

wait quietly before God,

for my hope is in Him.

Psalm 62:5

Wait Quietly

To wait quietly before the Lord is to sit in

His presence and learn to hope in Him

only. When we do this, we will then learn

to work from our rest, rather than

seeking to rest from our work.

Be still in the presence of the Lord,

and wait patiently for Him to act...

Psalm 37:7

Wait Patiently

Patience is the willingness

to walk at another's pace.

Learning to wait for God to act means

being willing to walk at God's pace;

to fall in line with

the unhurried, confident gait of our Father.

I am counting on the Lord;

yes, I am counting on Him.

I have put my hope in His word.

Psalm 130:5

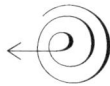

Wait Expectantly

There is a difference

between waiting with expectations—

a preconceived notion of HOW God will act—

and waiting expectantly—

an attitude of confident trust and satisfaction

with whatever God will choose to do.

Wait patiently for the Lord.

Be brave and courageous.

Yes, wait patiently for the Lord.

Psalm 27:14

Wait Courageously

Courage is fear that has said its prayers.

When you are terrified,

you don't run from your fears,

but you name and face them

with faith that God can overcome them.

It is learning to replace anxiety with worship.

Be Still

From Psalm 46

In the times of trouble

In the face of natural disasters

Earthquakes

Crumbling glaciers

Rising oceans

Be still

In the presence of God

In the home of God

In the eternal

Unassailable

City of God

In times of societal upheaval

crashing economies

national uncertainties

Be still

Be still

Because God speaks in absolute Power and

Authority.

Because He Is Here.

Because He is our Protection

Because Kings and Kingdoms still bow to Him

Because He is STILL.

He is still supreme.

He is STILL Sovereign.

He is still the...

..."In the beginning" God

..."And God said" God

..."I AM" God

..."Lord of Heavens Armies" God.

Be still because

He is STILL God.

*What people are saying about **A Word to the Wise**...*

"Jason Perry is wise beyond his years.

His books, devotionals, and daily posts

are like putting logs on spiritual fire.

His words of godly wisdom are fuel for my day."

Babbie Mason, Gospel Artist, Author, Entrepreneur

"As I read Jason Perry's inspirational/devotional,

I joyfully find both the Living Word of God and a

Powerful quote that ENERGIZES me to make a

RIGHT NOW application in my life that day of what I

just DIGESTED from his thought-provoking content!"

Sharan Trotter, Mental Health Therapist/

Counselor

"Jason Perry helps us gaze more deeply into

Scripture and helps us have greater spiritual

sensitivity."

Dr. Vince Bacote, Professor of Theology

*What people are saying about **A Word to the Wise**...*

"I appreciate Pastor Jason's ability to nuance the revelation and connection to Scripture with practical application. The ending quotes he provides offer unique stick-to-itness! I'm helped!"

Anthony R. Thomas, Pastor

"The Lord has always blessed Jason with insights that have caused me to pause, examine the Word and adjust my perceptions. These "snippets" are always powerful and thought-provoking. I also trust his words because I know they flow from a heart of love and Christ-centered humility."

Miian Bittenbender, Life Coach

What Jason pens is pithy, practical, powerful and often prophetic!

Tim Roehl, President, Fit and Flourish

Big ideas can come in little packages.

We don't always need a whole book or a full

sermon to communicate a significant truth.

A Word to the Wise

grew from a seed planted by some of my

students who encouraged me to capture

pithy statements I would make that helped them

to understand large concepts.

While every complex thought

can be teased out in greater detail,

there is usually a single idea at its core

that really gets to the heart of the matter.

Jason Perry *is a pastor, author and life coach*

who is passionate about helping people

live life to the fullest.

Made in the USA
Monee, IL
25 September 2023

61c7120b-b471-41a0-8f5c-015f886db76dR01